MW01253504

Plimsoll Lines

Donia Mounsef

Crossroads Poetry Series
Three Fires Confederacy Territory
Windsor, Ontario, Canada

First Edition. February 2018

Library and Archives Canada Cataloguing in Publication

Mounsef, Donia, author
        Plimsoll lines / Donia Mounsef.

Poems.
ISBN 978-1-988214-21-4 (softcover)

        I. Title.

PS8626.O8476P55 2017   C811'.6   C2017-907519-5

Book Layout: D.A. Lockhart
Book Cover: D.A. Lockhart
Cover Image: "Lofoten' by Diane Chisholm

Published in the United States of America and Canada by

 Urban Farmhouse Press
www.urbanfarmhousepress.com

The Crossroads Poetry Series is a line of books that showcases established and emerging poetic voices from across North America. The books in this series represent what the editors at UFP believe to be some of the strongest voices in both American and Canadian poetics. *Plimsoll Lines* is the ninth book in this series.

Printed in Adobe Garamond Pro font

CONTENTS

FLOOD TIDE:

NEAP TIDE:

FALLING TIDE

Plimsoll Lines I: Keel

Rope me to your bollard,
near a sea shaped like your body,
an ocean without waves
where offerings of tobacco
to forgotten ancestors
go unanswered,
in a mid-autumn that does not know
how to come.

An imaginary smell of seaweed,
a capricious falling tide forming
in the folds of your eyelids
to rescue my lonely thoughts,
from memory's ballast keel,
washing names of places,
stealing kisses, pirates
with contraband cargo.

How do we find each other
aboard a vessel made of sound?
where Plimsoll lines are drawn with sighs,
in the darkness of a west
that used to be wild
spread over the Canadian shield,
stowaways we remain
on a sunken boat,
dredging a mucky basin
for a rope buried in the sediments

of one's history,
a frayed loop in three strand weave
pulling specters of desire
closer together.

Plimsoll Lines II: What is Home?

The rope has become a collar,
tied to a fake trap door on a stage
with no escape,
abandoned ghost light,
twisted like an old telephone cord
where awful words are said
that no dictionary of love can define.

Tears collect by the threshold
of a door that closes more often than it opens,
endurable enduring grief
familiar only to doorways,
where a knife tilts the hinges, stabs speech –
in what language does silence speak?
Broken threads of a spider's web shaped like
love between two damaged people.
We are so lost we can't even find the ground
we are stomping on in anger.
Pounding the asphalt of Terminal City,
I imagine treading in the monochromatic winter,
disappear into the night blue of a nearby ocean,
lean my heavy limbs against
an abandoned log to call home.

What is home?
but the circle of her arms,
the woman who lies in the other room,
the total stranger,
the one who loves you,
the one who loves you knot.
What is home?
but the dirty rounded corners

of a tousled duffel bag
left on an unfriendly terrace,
one dreary winter night.

Plimsoll Lines III: Jericho Beach

I wake up not from a night's sleep
but from the daze of missing you.
I surge to my feet,
rush to the slate window,
to the north,
the frozen city stretches its arms,
quietly to the banks of an invisible river,
rising in a heap of solid water,
pushing the pang of exile against
the frosty bedrock I call home.

I look up at the blue midnight
to find you sailing in the sky,
your body scattered on a platter of stars,
your lips savoring the twilight.
I ask the void up above
how to find my way back to you
point to your location on
a map blanched by light years,
eyes blinded by bleeding fears.

A flickering flame rising from the fog
at New Year's Day,
in the crisp coastal winter,
where Jericho Beach
swoons into Spanish Banks –
a tepid wave permeates the inlet at your feet,
an echo of flight in your eyes
speaks the language of depth,
the depth of language.

Your image printed on a radiant green

stretches across the land mass,
over mounts and rivers,
journey with the northern lights
to paint a mural on the walls of my heart –
this unsinkable muscle,
thrown overboard a pirate's ship
floating toward a dim lighthouse,
tended by ghosts of lost sailors
yearning for a piece of earth
to rest their weary bodies,
looking for love in transient places,
in the camber of waves,
in the emptiness of door frames,
in the frailty of fire escapes,
in the dithering of a gypsy tent
tattooed with longing for a sign
of tenderness you withhold,
as if you are saving for the day
the floodgate opens and your warmth
rushes out, scrambled with desire
that refuses to be beaten.

Angel Glacier – Mount Edith Cavell

Angel,
a glacier no more,
a rock de-formation,
reverberating sounds of ancient times,
before language was placed under suspicion,
a lone hawk flies low beneath the earth
its wings etch stone like a scar etches memory.

> At the moment when crystals liquesce into dust,
> ice flows punctuate a prehistoric lake,
> faint wind rattles a glassy water surface,
> a flawed circle drawn with the many failures of unity,
> as if to chastise the imperfection of time.

A carving hand caresses
an imagined line in the center of the valley,
the switchblade of geological evanescence,
painfully separates the glacier from the rock,
matter from history,
me from you.

> Departing boats
> unmooring unfriendly harbors,
> ancient ice, both living and dead,
> hanging and falling,
> dances in the shaded crevices of silence.

Whittled chronicles in melted stone,
a cataract inhabiting the retina of time,
a pile of words forlorn on a worn-out rock,
blind bats gliding in the caves of meaning.

Like aging glaciers,
all writing is a form of separation.

Liquid Caresses

when you are landlocked
you mistake a sandstorm
for sea gale
a wild rose
for a sting ray
a rattle snake
for shimmering seaweed
a streak of northern light
for wet blue neap tide
a prairie snow heap
for a beach scarp
lonely people
in front of their TV sets
for derelict vessels
in abandoned harbors
cracked clay earth
for sinuous sand dunes
prairie breeze
for landward uprush
at the wave break

and you wait
in desperate drought
for rain to come
and awaken your senses
to wash away your thirst
float in an ocean
of liquid caresses

11

Beirut Cafés

Beirut cafés are filled with old men who have nothing left to say;
careless of the Arabic pop music playing in the background.
They look around with fixed eyes
for that waiter who will bring them a small *rakweh*,
fragrant with cardamom coffee,
and a *finjan*,
"*wah'ad ahweh murrah, mitl hal zaman*"
["one coffee, black – bitter like this life"]
they say in a raspy voice,
just one...

They wilt along the dried flowers resting
in a reused bottle vase.
They wish they had more time to finish that game,
to find that last crossword puzzle,
to answer a call from a son whose voice they ache to hear.
"*wledak barra?*" one asks the other
"*eh walla, killun barra*"
"yes, sadly, all my children are abroad"
"*barra*" is abroad but also without,
a code word for those without whom one never learns to live,
a daily reminder of when they left,
walked onto boat bridges
in the night,
between two cease-fires, never to return.

They wish they had a spring in their step to catch
that grandchild they never met,
who keeps running away from them,
in their dream filled with pastel longing.
They worry as much about the humidity,
as the world crumbling around them,

in the heat of Gemmayzeh,
broken by waves of savage bombing,
and audacious street fighters
who thought they were making history,
when it unmade them...

They have fought at least three wars,
climbed at least 50 towers when the power was out,
without resting;
then resting more and more at each floor,
as the years went by.
They whispered sweet nothing in many lovers' ears,
hurt and been hurt by love come and gone.
Danced in and out of many frames
of happiness.

But time...

When the day surrenders,
they resign themselves to leaving through the defaced oak door,
lift their bodies with heavy palms off the distressed cedar table,
dreading the uphill,
and the silence of a loveless home,
abandoned by all the children stolen by *hijra*.
All those loved ones they held scantily,
not knowing that their old man's grip is not strong enough
against the tyranny of maps.

Their present, only a past reshaped by departures,
time falling apart around them,
in an exploding hourglass,
marking hours, minutes, seconds
of the ruinous island they have become,
littered with shipwrecks of their former selves.

They change their mind,
sit down again,
hiding their sorrow in the wrinkles
under their squinting eyes,
shifting like the raggedy table,
aged with the Middle-East sun and stomping hands,
playing backgammon,
"*sheish beish*"…

Bonfire

We lit a bonfire by the sea,
to burn all that is left of our story -
years we spent telling
chronicles of disappearance,
looking for ourselves in the bellowing tide,
gleaning meaning from stone,
snake tongued, shell shocked,
trapped in the underwater museums
of our own inner relics.
You wanted to resolve the gravitational
force of the moon,
the amphidromic rhythm of oceans
on tidal range,
find the ghost ship, lost
in the impossible geography between us.
All I wanted was to lay my head in your lap,
rescue the thrush from the scalding ashes.
I have come in from a long march of exiles,
twined myself into you,
furred nakedness looking for heat
in the frigid northwest coast winter.
We bundled the past like a newspaper ball
and tossed it in the fire,
as it flamed, holy inscriptions
emerged to tell us that
making blankets from the abyss
will not keep us warm.

Homeland

Although I was never very patriotic,
I visit your body like a homeland,
it smells of incense
                    inside you,
of solemn layers upon layers
of argyle and clay,
cedar bark baked in a brazing Levantine sun,
a stone fire of lava.

You stand blocking the way
before Sunday,
an eternal Sabbath
keeps me hanging from your autumn eyes,
captured
        in one glance,
        the grief of many departures.

My hand quivers on the small of your back,
sketching tactile meadows
where borders are unguarded,
        where barbed wire does not tear apart intruders.

With an ear resting on your chest, I listen to your breath
        a soldier breaking from battle,
        it speaks of a time beyond the present,
        in a language I alone can understand.

When the injustice of geography tears us apart,
I leave your body like one leaves a homeland
        with an inaudible lament
        a pinch of dirt in my pocket,
and a single blue tear as a promise of return.

This is the House I: "Guests on the Sea"
In memory of Noel

"Guests on the sea. Our visit is short."
-Mahmoud Darwish

This is the house strong muscles
built in the wind
while Katrina plundered the coast
leaving haunted shacks
filled with women who were not there,
the fruit of knowledge located in flooded air
water sliced thin by skipping stones.
Elsewhere the game has different rules,
the wise man said,
taking pictures of the horizon
of a lonesome sea rock
where his young son
lost to cancer
may or may not have appeared,
a game of precision in Trinidad
where force is not prized.

This is the house that strong muscles
built on water, under the sun
between love and back ache,
in a liquid bed where kisses cling
to underside of feather pillows
mumbling on erratic quilts,
where laughter flows from uneven walls.

If she had her way
she would bring the beach sand to our yard,

we would roll in white crystals
like wayward dogs in grass,
pleasure seekers
in the arms of valiant ecstasy.
Boardwalk dunes
would be the way to our kitchen,
and a million fast swimming fishlings
would nibble at our feet.

How can a house
be the size of the ocean?

This is the House II: "Upon the Sand"

"Safe upon the solid rock the ugly houses stand:
Come and see my shining palace built upon the sand!"
                                                    -Edna St Vincent Millay

This is the house weary muscles tore apart
with indelible farewells,
given away
one summer night from a distance
to a total stranger,
for it could no longer house our fears…
letting go of what we never had
showing pictures to curious eyes
of the peach room,
the Isle of Capri,
the cubist painting, our life has become.

This is the house that could not speak,
under each cedar board
laid down by Winchester gun factory workers,
a story was written
with sweat and tears,
words like termites wedged
in its doorframes.
Furtive rain drops drizzle a wet morning,
in a dry bed where a body sketch
is outlined with sweat marks,
grief echoes from crawl spaces,
the aged frame tilts toward death.

Abandoned houses lay
at the bottom of one's mind,
like ribs of a boat on the ocean floor,

sunk in a rage
because they could no longer
save us from reckless desire,
where torn sails,
ghosts of wreck divers
search for air and pure weightlessness.

How can a house
be the size of a suitcase?

Atlantis

Poetry is a country that does not exist,
wiped off the map in the rage of a fascist monster
who wanted everything to have an answer.
Atlantis of language,
we go digging for meaning foundered there
grieving at the bottom of a sea
of atonement,
beneath the pillars of Hercules,
nostalgic for whether anything existed, not sure
of its inhabitants, the color of their skin,
the size of their feet.
We dive like Adrienne Rich
into the wreck of words,
scratch ourselves with their slivers.
Sailors of the in-between,
torpedoes of truth,
we carry sunken boats on our aching backs,
earth shakers like Poseidon, we plot
islands of doubt, arouse seas of uncertainty,
make love in empty hulls, fornicate
with adjectives laying in the transom –
heaps of discarded verbs shrouding in gunwales,
adverbs qualify or change, repeat the uniqueness
singularize the third hidden side of an invisible freeboard,
objects inside the binary shroud
unfinish the sharp edges of a broken mast.

Nothing that is poetic is complete,
this dead art of living corpses,
a language prostitute,
we hire for batting an eye at us,
her wings stolen from fallen angels, dead sailors,

thump, shake fists at,
stomp under our feet,
caress, fondle, rub against,
shield from inscrutable silence,
the unbearable numbness between two bodies,
the unspeakable terror of definitive meaning.
Poetry is
losing Atlantis in our effort to find it.

Listen

I enter a luminous labyrinth, your body
turned to incandescent light,
in the silence of the coastal nightfall,
interrupted by sparks in your eyes,
waiting by the door.
I had been to hell and back,
I swam in rivers of veins and pains,
and tended to irregular heartbeats,
I found a home between two exiles.

I unbutton a reluctant shirt,
ease the hurt of distance,
gently tracing the way to your concealed heart,
lying motionless in your thorax,
inside daring lace and a red bra.
Ghosts of previous touches I left adrift
on the shores of your incensed sea.
In the wetness under the surface tension,
debris of madness and loss,
dancing around your drowsy body,
I trace with the fervor of a map maker:
maps are only visible because of their margins.

In the drifts of continents,
with their infinite dereliction of touch,
where eloped passions fade with abandonment,
no matter how deep anger is,
love is always deeper,
an ocean floor with sunken prows,
mysterious fish
rushing around as if to say:
"linger here, stretched, and silent,

listen to the murmur of skin to skin,
the stone bracketed laments
of tattered hearts,
– just listen."

EBB TIDE

Stolen Land I: The Currie Barracks

All land is stolen,
every home is someone else's exile,
every step toward a free ground
is someone else's brick trowel,
spreading mortar for a pallid wall,
every dreamy gaze at a celestial star
is someone else kneeling down to kiss a virgin soil,

and claim, clamoring
we claim, they claim,
a land claim is not just ink on paper,
it's a blood rushing through veins,
the rain, a desert long awaits for,
a refugee's purple dream of resting after a long march,
harsh winters and distant shores.
And we hide from history,
our shameful plows burrowing into the abyss of purity,
shut un-sentinelled lighthouses
with faintly disappearing lights,
the flight of Icarus toward the sun,
melting wings, open arms,
who forgot how it feels to embrace
after a long awaited return.

Stolen Land II: Bite and Hold

Decommissioned, treaty 7, treated, mistreated,
a first nation had no land,
only asbestos contamination.
Give them the old barracks with unexploded ordinances,
and pictures of generals with head regalia tributing the queen.
Here the troops were trooping
fruitless menaces with
bite and hold, bitten and held
against a prairie wind unfit for habitation.
Places we bury the past without headstones.
Here we left a dying father who suppressed all his tears,
locked them in his hands, spreading an aching touch
over mountains and seas.
Here we left a sharp pencil mark on the wall,
next to where the shrapnel hit.
Here we left the inward side of a heart
on a sidewalk broken at the corner.
There, children are signing artillery shells
to send to other children across the border.
Cluster bombs opened the clear blue sky,
phosphorous, a poison fruit unleashed
with the guilt of Occupation.
The people hunkered down counting
air raids and seconds to impact.
Here drums quit pulsating their skin to listen
to the moaning of the uncounted dead.

And we endure in congested lands
for the intention of occupation,
in over-crowded refugee camps for rationed stale meals,
in vacant hearts for the intention of love.
Like a nail endures the intention of a hammer,

a full moon also endures prismatic light polishing its edges,
and an aged sea vessel endures the salting of its ribs,
rusting its hinges to charred orange.
Here, where even breathing takes courage,
we hold and bite the pain of leaving, the pain of settling,
the pain of giving up,
giving in,
giving over what never belonged to us.
We pack a picture in lieu of the scent of jasmine, and wonder
why can't we conceive of land as a gift –
a beach corner we borrow to spread a tattered towel over,
enjoy fleetingly until the sun sets
and all the mermaids go home?
Why is our relationship to land structured around ownership?

Ferdaws

[The Arabic word "ferdaws": paradise, and garden.
From the Persian, "pairi", around, and "diz", wall]

Sitting in ashen solitude,
looking around the walls of paradise,
in the heavenly stillness of her dark eyes,
a past stares at me from the heated tip of a machine gun,
dreaming of wet rocks by the sea,
hiding beneath the weightlessness of uncombed shores.

Her lugubrious eyes turned keel of our unsteady vessel,
throwing questions at her like javelins,
disturbing the beautiful certainty of her radical "yes".
I had given up on finding her,
in that moment when I knew
that my soul was picked out of a line up,
herded against a bloodied wall,
facing a firing squad of affect,
striking emptiness like a match,
momentary burning light in the deep hollows of memory.

Love, a bouquet of nothingness I clutch to the chest,
a poem no one will ever read,
an invisible barrier between heaven and earth.
Our tragic irony, when, exhausted,
we cross the finish line
at the end of a marathon of emotion,
grasping orphaned feelings,
curled up in a ball on the floor,
sensations like coins falling out of pockets,
as we run away from a body
that so longs to be blooming into ours.

But we wait,
standing at the edge of a pool in trepidation,
littered with paint chips we call hope
counting the cracks in the mosaics,
the ransom paid for our freedom to love.
We lie down in the bottom of the empty cement,
play dead in a dry cemetery of abandon,
peer over our own decorated coffin,
itemizing all the ways we could've loved better,
wishing to be born in a *ferdaws* without walls.

The Iceman

Found thousands of years later,
an icy, iceman icycling on the side of melting icefields,
betrayed by global warming and savage development.
We broke the cycle with our worship of money,
fluctuation betting,
speculation bloodletting,
on acid rain, black gold, brown angel dust.
We tore down trees to build houses,
tore down houses to build highways to bigger houses,
tore down bigger houses to build more exclusive compounds,
tore down more exclusive compounds
to build the largest bunker to contain our fear.

We are alone on a piece of earth that does not belong to us,
afraid of other salesmen like us, selling fake titles,
buying distance measured in scorched earth,
charred skeletons, imprints of human skin.
And when the earth coughed, telling us it "can't breathe,"
we dispatched militarized police,
sent down like Orpheus to its belly, choke-held it,
ripped its guts into tar,
buried the emerald sea and danced on liquid graves,
gravely, aggravatingly, grievingly.
The boiling temperature turns reality into politics,
politics into fiction,
warning systems, NORAD on windy islands inlets,
incredible inkpots,
high water marks, long dried up and shriveled old cliffs,
the earth, our second skin,
a sepulcher for our sins.

Emerald vermillion deposits block the arteries

of our arcane blood,
prophecies of water return when the flood comes raging,
splitting icebergs,
at the feet of the Pacific, drenched with heartbreak,
the yogi from India forewarned the storm:
"disturbing a sleeping man will piss off the gods,
don't find him, don't sell him, don't weep for him,
don't expose him to the sun,
blazing suns a frozen heart don't warm."

Hémiplégie

The early morning dew shines over sleepy hills,
in the background,
dreary mountains and concrete,
in the foreground,
construction cranes swallowed refugee camps.
Beauty and ugliness cohabit my curtailed sight,
the muggy heat is lurking,
around the corner in East Beirut,
the carob tree where the young man hung himself,
has turned to charcoal at the wall of Sioufi garden.
A dog lies buried there,
among a child's broken dreams.
I carried you like empty gun shells,
an ailing mother who stopped walking
of fear of reaching the other side,
over rivers and mountains,
inside crackling phone lines,
on beaches where you left me alone,
to fight the intrepid tide,
in stairways where you pushed me to leave,
while your eyes implored me to stay.

You said, I only know how to speak about love,
what use is having a language for love I alone understand?
what is the point of having time,
when death is lurking in closets
shut on a dead man's clothes?

Words are like gems stuck in the mud,
a kaleidoscopic mirror stripped of its reflections.
Clear fog and a wet flame,
a body half paralyzed by deception,

wanting to live and die at once,
healing and deep-rooted scars,
engraved on bedroom walls,
turned to hospital rooms,
a theatre of operation –
the doctor said *hémiplégie*, a term I thought I knew
I tried to pull out from my inner dictionary,
half of it means "half",
the other half must be "paralysis" –
the analytical mind says,
half of me is paralyzed,
I don't know anymore which half loves you,
and which one aches for the sunshine alone –
a prisoner of what could be,
the executioner of what was,
even this language is no longer mine,
hémiplégie, I forgot I knew,
stuck here in my throat with an "h" that is silent.

Jabal Sannin

Abu Youssef stared at it from his unfinished roof,
a restive place under tall pine trees that spit their cones,

in a programmable rhythm,
at the pace of his old grand-fatherly fingers rounding

another circle of his worry beads.
Under weeping willows and crimson pomegranate juice,

laying on a Damascene marble stone.
If he had one wish, he would embrace Mount Sannin in his arms,

along with his many children, he raised alone
when their mother died birthing their last.

He loved her so much,
he never remarried,

he moved train tracks to remember her every day.
Facing west from the small village of Rayak,

that always looks auspiciously serene
even under a stormy sky.

The Beqaa is where the valley flirts with heavens,
resting in a chiaroscuro of pink and orange

redolent with thyme and place.
He mumbles to himself: "*ma ba'rif*"

"I don't know" –
the old man who knows so much.

36

Occupy
A performance poem

99 percent occupy the street,
downbeat we compete to unseat,
repo man coming to repossess the beat,
generation with or without inflation,
complacent minds,
unsigned treaties, defaced graffiti from here to Tahiti.
We tweet like tweetie bird, pictures of dead herd and suicidal teenagers,
constituents, constituency, cons, tits, and truancy,
the Obama mamas, colorful pajamas, bearded allamas,
the American dream, bursting at the seam,
protected by riot police, keeping the peace to increase
profit, acquit criminals with sleaze,
hit the crowd in the knees,
lock us all up throw away the keys,
break democracy's back with a baton,
from here to Gabon.
A cross beam between real rage and blowing off steam,
ice cream flavored banana republic,
pliers tightening on tight white tuxedos dancing the night away,
deregulated regulations, surfing pipelines under the sea
of disappointment, torment the masses declassify classes,
amass fortune cookies, sell your life to a bookie,
sign the decree that no one can see.
Occupy the incumbents, the bents in the road to uncertain futures,
the sutures holding the ailing political body together,
when they locked Tito Kayak up and let Strauss Kahn go,
"so"? said the reporter sipping on Bordeaux,
consuming plea bargains,
spewing jargon, carbon footprints,
harassing Jesus in the garden of Eden
getting even,

in Sweden there is a price for the Nobel peace prize,
you don't have to play nice just roll the dice and pay,
the market will take care of everything,
but not of your ailing mother.
"Black lives matter" served on a platter,
scatter, or be peppered sprayed if you stayed down-ward dog,
leap frog bridges to nowhere, holiday spirit, the walk, the talk,
the stock selling girls in Bangkok,
unlock the cinder block, draw a chalk line where
the student protestor laid under
sergeant pepper's feet.
Invincible robo-cops, with shiny props, eating Monsento crops,
United Nations, work stations, charlatan divinations,
call centers, crooked lenders, repeat offenders,
traffic surveillance, hypnotic trance, danse macabre,
wind and water turbine energy synergy,
CCTV poison ivy, we vie on megaphones,
to down weaponized drones.
Bloomberg Greenberg Cronenberg
are only louder if we let them.
Occupy the occupied occupation pre-occupying
seduction suction fluxion,
satirical humor and late-night talk shows.
Hide your liberal heart, your broken leg, your queer chandelier,
dive in empty pools, outdated rules,
stuff your face with halva from Istanbul,
fight fraud, firing squad and the kingdom of god,
teleprompters, captors, incapsulators,
mars rovers, the new planet 6000 light years away.

If machines can find their way to a new galaxy,
why can't we find the way to each other?

Concrete

*"Did you know about the rose that grew
from the concrete crack?"*

-Tupac Shakur

they built a wall
in the land of Jesus
to give shape to partition
to give color to hate
to make separation concrete

        daring travelers climbed it
        lifting their ramshackle bags
        and their neatly dressed children
        above their heads
        like white flags
        "don't shoot"

soldiers gazed
at its imperfection
put out their cigarette butts
in its crevices
to cover the scent
of oregano and mint
growing timidly in its fissures

        we too built walls
        when we could no longer
        look at each other
        and soon stabbed holes into them
        for snipers to sneak
        the beak of their Barretts
        and aim at a presumed enemy

who looks like us
who smells like us
who walks the same earth
with the same shoes
who goes to bed
at night clutching the same hunger

        ten round magazines
        ten lives
        ten children
        who play the same games we play
        dream the same dreams
        collect the same seashells
        hold them to their ears
        the same way we do
        to listen to a distant ocean
        where our ancestors
        silently lament
        the ever growing
        abyss between us

walls grow inside you
until your soul becomes
a pile of bricks
your eyes square up
like bathroom tiles
when you look at your neighbors
you only see the pieces
that make them different

        walls cannot protect you
        they are not solid
        they are quilts
        they tell multiple stories
        form a moving shade

of light and darkness
inside your perfect picture of sameness

a wall is a wish
you only know you
did not wish
once you stand beneath
and gaze at its
insurmountable height
like a nightmare
in a cotton-filled dream
like a coin tossed
in a dried-up fountain
a wall is a mistake
a rose growing in the concrete

"Distressed Submersion Diagnostics"
A performance poem

They warned us against moral deregulation,
and went ahead and did it anyway
deregulating policies
policing regular irregularities
the rules of law on reality TV
spread habeas corpuses in morgues full of dead ethics
road kill on the interstates
between Wall Street and main street
and ran them over and over again
with a six wheeler
carrying expired dog food
subdued the last frontier
the plagued ghetto no one dares to set foot in
because Mary had a little lamb but no love
and OJ had a dirty glove
and Ben Laden was watching porn
a thorn in the thigh of puritanical America
she wasn't in the mood, she turned him
into fish food

they made us question what we see
misunderstand what we comprehend
disbelieve what we know to be or not be
what is or isn't true
is a T still a T?
the O? is it still an oh
R you sure?
and who crosses the other T?
is it U?
aRen't you
Effing-efficient?

it is not what you think you see
coercion measures to protect you and me
in the post-mortem Gestapotential dictionary of
chemicals sprayed are for splashy interrogation
fingers chopped are for enhanced compulsion
and who needs ten anyway?
Kidnapping is just a special form of rendition
but for the kids rendered no napping is allowed
it is called sleep management
loud heavy metal music
if Jimi Hendrix knew his music is used
by the few, the brave
turning in his grave with
the sleep deprived
take five
test drive exceptional positions
arms stretched tied to the ceiling
heightened techniques
obliques odalisque
collected like antiques
unique boutiques
for international pressure shoppers
mild non-injurious physical contact
cell packed like sardines
broken limbs held between
a rock and a charred place

the kid from Milwaukee never meant to go that far
he thought he knew who his enemies are
in that video game
where waterboarding is showbiz
just another way to level-up
a pop quiz
distressed submersion diagnostics
the left or right button?
push once to attack

twice to defend
turn the middle dial to suffocate hope
for the best
until it confesses to being despair in disguise
the Geneva Convention is written on toilet paper
the more it piles up the more it stinks
the sphinx has a riddle
strapped to the chest of language
suicided itself
on the outside walls of silence
the fat cow at the stock exchange
the only building that still had power during the storm
stay warm
reform swarm the bullies
who run the planet and claim chastity at the gates of heaven
stay in the path of the shit storm we call politics
forget the gloom, buy more
the cathedral of democracy rumbles
stumbles
crumbles
filled with soldiers of doom
where will they strike next?

Orient This!

I will not talk to you about the East,
the Orient, the Levant
the fertile crescent,
about burnt libraries, Talmudic stories
Dead Sea Scrolls,
faggy Alexanders, bloody Caesars,
trolls and death tolls.

I will not portray for you bearded terrorists,
madmen mullahs,
veiled women, failed revolutions,
grand illusions,
purge you from the guilt
of shooting at the other, alone
from the eye of a drone.

I will not tell you about the alphabet,
imminent threat, astronomical achievements
alchemy, algorithms,
and the Robayyat.

I will not entertain you with Shaherezade,
tickle your ears with 1001 strident arias,
feed your hysteria, take you on a ride
with a war bride, on the camelback of meaning
and regale you with figs
from the eternal tree of desert symbolism.

I will not weave you a magic carpet,
with braided synonyms,
vivid colors,
excite you with epics of Gilgamesh,
give you answers to your burning questions,
bloodied generals,
hip dancers,
jabbing side to side,
to the silent tunes of voyeurism.

I will not make you decorations,
with thick lines drawn on silky fabric,
to affix to your white walls,

because you already possess all that.

Measured
An anti-performance poem

> "It's a measured response." Canadian Prime Minister Stephen
> Harper's answer, when asked at a press conference what he thinks
> of Israel's bombing of Lebanon during the July War, 2006.

"Measured"
the politician agreed with the anonymous journalist
chewing on the news feed
waving his fist while getting pissed
splice to a camera eye descending from the sky
over the rubble of Tyr
where the grey dust looks austere

cut to a hero playing Robert de Nero
hiding in ground zero
in camouflage fatigue
cultivating intrigue
looking through binoculars
while smoking big fat Cuban cigars

measured sympathy
a form of terror
reactionary statements writ with error
lives traded on far away stock-exchanges
blue helmets paraded
but no peace to be kept
the keepers slept in the heat of July

counting the dead
draped in white, green and red
a cedar lies on top of small coffins
children who never had the time
to play under their national tree
a war raged
the media caged
a tsunami upstaged
fitting to ignore
the earth boiled

the airwaves filled with verbal fecundity
the opium of the measured masses
and waxed beach asses

'*anqoudiya*, Arabic for poison fruit
clusters of light to reflect the bomber's loneliness
in a world where peace took a vow of silence
where violence speaks louder than a church bell
who has the luxury to be measuring
heat in hell

the politician sent an airplane
a measured flight to inspect a bomb site
a gesture so contrite
where two people boarded
and were soon discarded on the tarmac
as soon as the cameras left for the night

measured
press conference
under false pretense
with a lot of suspense
mouths speaking
eyes peeking
no sounds are heard
tongues dipped in the vaccine of complacency
trapped in a gigantic throat
between the cartilage and the thyroid
self-righteous beast
ignorant of the east
getting drunk on petro
spewing bullshit for ammo

how can you tell
what's measured
when you live in a shell
that covers the smell
a land of warfare cupid
where your bombs are smart
and politicians stupid?

A City without Walls

"We protect ourselves
against most things,
but against death
we live in a city without walls"
                    -Epicurus

I pass them every day as I run to Third Beach
and back listening to Arabic pop music,
three crosses on the northern wall of the vacant piscine,
moving along the dead cement
of an empty winter pool flirting with the Salish Sea.
I slow down, a hesitant foot in sand, then sprint ahead,
I see the attraction of the void, a choppy silent film,
unsynchronized shadows of those who left early,
mindless vessels of the storm they left behind.

Flashing messages in the dusk drenched coast,
where pigeons and seagulls jostle over
dirty plastic slides battered by a harsh northwest winter,
a deserted sign: "Men Working"
kips in the belly of the tiled cave,
dreaming of summer fickleness and children's laughter.
The Pacific is calm,
its waves beckon gently,
a reminder of our lot, the lonely living,
knocking on death's door, not expecting an answer.

Besides Jesus (even his return was disputed),
no one has ever come back to reassure us
that a distorted black cross is just
two lines marking swimming lanes,
in a city without walls,
separating the living from the dead,
at nightfall.

FLOOD TIDE

Asunder I: Where the Stress Falls

"The beauty of the world has two edges, one of laughter,
one of anguish, cutting the heart asunder."
                                        - Virginia Woolf

Your hands gesture,
cutting the air with deep motion,
emotion on your face,
your words stumble
race, stagger, slip, squint,
rush out to me,
like pressured waters,
bright blue, temple veins,
cherry red, scorched earth,
sanguine, sinuous, serpentine
shipwrecks on the shores of meaning.
And I am a faded autumn sun,
lost in your foreign sea,
trying to decode signals, and
where the stress falls,
        between the cracks in the wall
        of your body syntax.

I give up trying to understand,
get naked, slip into your warmth,
your cavernous heat burns my fingers,
I linger, meditate at the threshold of your flesh,
blindfold your demons,
track the fissure in the silence
of your breasts.
More is said
between breaths.
A mantra written on the walls of her heart:
"hold on to the woman
who can so deeply fall asleep
in your arms, from
        exhaustion of having to explain
        why she so needs to be held."

Asunder II: The Draft Took it Down

what did she say?
what did I hear?
why do we wonder?
why do we break
the heart asunder?
the heart is under,
sinking below the bridge
without a raft, the draft took it down,
        with the captain,
        laughing hysterically at his spectacular loss.

What you want,
and what you can't have
is the source of your pain.
I know your pain,
like the darkness knows the ditch,
the rain knows the gutter,
the dog knows his collar.
Your body relaxes,
softens, tempers, dilates,
lightens into elusive sleep,
aided by the flawless darkness in your window,
and the sound proofing
of fears into dreams,
a perfect conversion into a land
where you are understood,
without speaking,
where your words walk
without crutches on the floor boards,
without creaking,
        where the heart is whole
        and not asunder.

Auguste

We decided we could only have an imaginary dog,
we named him Auguste.

He was a shepherd-heeler cross, your favorite breed,
tempered and smart, gentle and agile.

He took us for walks, retrieved discus and delusions.
He could jump higher than a horse, run faster than a jaguar.

He would put a paw on you to calm you down, when agitated,
stare at you until you return to your writing.

He was perfect for our imperfections
– the whole canine yard.

One day, Auguste ran away from home,
vanished into thin air and thick brush,

in a forest of indistinct dreams,
left us his imaginary blue collar by the door,

chewed as if to mark love with
the permanence of karyotype;

a dental record of durable regret,
a silent bark compressed in a circle of sorrow.

In a broken shell of home inhabited by phantoms of dogs past,
his picture in an empty frame on the fridge,

and the glow of his ghostly smile to remind us
that we can lose even what we never had.

Body Politics

What body will you offer me tonight?
The one resting in a hammock on the Canadian Shield,
or the wounded shell with heavy limbs,
hazed by cheap wine,
hiding, defenseless behind a disheveled white shirt?
You take a risk with looking, wanting, coveting,
breasts exposed, deposed, disclosed,
dormant nipples perk up to the thought –
unthink!

You were never good at assessing risk,
I was never good at keeping records,
we know not to take what we can't give,
not to give what we can't keep, and yet
we raise a flag to our ravaged selves,
stake a territory in the occupied land of uncertainty,
summon our knights to battle,
melt steely armors, put it all on the line,
what's yours, what's mine,
fly away on rusty wings,
pimping our dreams to the demi-gods of the flesh,
a pantomime of endless body politics,
as the clock ticks,
desire lingers in withered time.

Narcissus

In the ice kingdom, rivers sleep in winter,
hibernate under blocks of cracked ice,
dreaming of warmth and wild runs,
to the other side of the great divide,
scraping glacial deposits to the Hudson Bay,
rest their chary beds until spring,
when they open their eyes,
awakened by the gods of the tundra,
jet under the surface,
tickling the frozen mass from beneath.
The south bank of the North Saskatchewan River
is a tropical garden,
a green ribbon where one finds
in the dead of winter
a northern maidenhair fern
veiled in darkness,
wrestling with the northern light
in a barren winter poplar,
a strident reverberation of a magpie,
watching over its empty nest
stretches its white noise
over the taciturn valley.

Stop to look at a strange plant
with green leaves,
frozen in the shape of an origami raven,
wings etched into the ice blanket,
wintery eyes spot something
moving under the surface, a liquid kaleidoscope
waiting to be reunited with solid matter,
gaze at the glassy sheet,
become a Narcissus,
bent down to kiss a water vision,
an emergent image falls into you, plaintive,
it whispers like Echo for eternity,
repeating words spoken into the undying gorge
yearning for love that would never be returned,
where the body disappeared
a flower is painfully growing in its place.

Not all Lava

Twisted words hung from the
blinds hiding all that is wrong
with this conversation,
you said
I said
you said
who said what when?
who used which tone why?
who hurt more who less?
who is under duress?
who got us into this mess?
who pulled the trigger first?
who is ready to burst?
who loaded the gun?
who eclipsed the sun?
why did we misunderstand
what we already understood?
why is there a hole where we once stood?
who let the gavel fall?
who shut the door, who built a wall?

There are two versions to every fight,
there are two wings to every flight,
or three or four or even more,
we can't nail it down we can't let it fly,
the story shifts, no matter who tries,
not all lava petrifies.

Friend or Foe

She wanted to know
if one day we could be friends,
I heard "foe" –
she said "stay" –
I gleaned "go" –
she said, "will I see you tomorrow" –
I heard, "I'm filled with sorrow" –
she said, "keep me company 'til the day breaks" –
I heard the earth shake,
familiar strangers in a disaster zone,
lone murmurs in her floorboards,
turned to tremors
at the epicenter of her heart,
death flares did us part.

I sat by the sea, on a mossy log, in the mist
made a list of all the languages
we did not speak,
the language of maybe,
the language of what ifs,
the language of dancing cliffs,
the language of quiet hieroglyphs.
I held fragments of her palliative speech
a burning wick in my hands,
in the space-time capsule,
of the end of passion,
where her portentous word demands to be heard,
all she said is "save me," and I heard "leave me."

Inhabited by memory's insurgence
against punctuation,
the past is a sea monster
buried in scorching parenthesis,
bracketed in the shadowy columns of Atlantis,
concealed in exclamation points,
a driver sleeping at the wheel of language
who could never explain
why she could never explain
the difference between a full stop

and an ellipsis.

I looked at the foamy water surface,
grateful that the sky hasn't fallen
from so much misunderstanding,
that the Coast Mountains still shimmer in the sun
draped with fresh snow,
that a single tree endures above the snowline,
that a bald eagle still glides from Brackendale
to the western horizon in geometric precision.
I buried you in the cavernous silence of my throat
with no memorial to commemorate our dead,
only a breath condensation forming in a frosty winter
to remind us that we were here,
and we breathed the same Salish air.

This Wing

This wing
wants to fly back

to where a nest breaks dawn,
where it all began,

a single bird's eye view of our fate,
flying over cities in ruins,

bombed out hospitals in Aleppo,
tattered buildings with their guts out,

where even rain drops stopped falling.
Gliding to the sole weeping willow,

standing sentry at a freshly dug out grave,
pruning scorched tree tops,

drawing smiles on a scarecrow's face,
spiked in a minefield of beautiful devastation.

This wing etched in stone
wants to fly.

A Water Skipper's Stone

The best love poems are
about the possibility of flight,
the phases of the moon,
the Arctic night, a ring found
in the melting snow in spring.

They are about an
illusion of lust,
the dust train tracks make
carrying refugees
to an uncertain future.

The suture that heals jagged
on the wrist,
the future fold of an origami hawk,
a sunray lifting the mist
surrounding shipwrecks.

About malfunctioning drones,
a religion that does not ask you to kneel,
a water skipper's stone
skimming the surface
of the unknown.

Painting breaches
in a border wall
where armies refuse to deploy,
a star in the Aquila constellation
named after a little boy.

Check

A performance poem

When you truly let go, the Buddha says
you give up the assurance of next,
the familiarity of last,
forsake the certainty of the past,
denounce impatient angst,
defy the duality of contrasts,
surrender passion,
ration emotion,
      drink the ashen grey of your vast shipwreck,
      sweep the floor deck,
      cut messy hair, check
      trim nails to the quick,
      check check,
you're clean,
an invincible machine, full of conviction
ready for your rendez-vous with affliction,
the invisible guest beating their fist at your table,
devouring your woes, between sips of expensive scotch,
and bites of what is left of your nails,
serving you your own head,
turning round and round on a circular plate,
of your own making,
relinquish the taking,
remove imaginary screens before your eyes,
no matter how much she tries,
she will always toss your words,
like a penny in the burning fire of oblivion,
heartless, she can make you dream the nightmare blue,
tattoo her picture on the inside of your skull,
with dirty needles and dried up ink,
sink your poems in a fountain of routine,
wipe the slate clean,
coddle the in-between,
cut the frayed rope, intervene
in the abandon at the edge of the cliff
elope the battered self,
      sit with it, check
      stay in the pain,

        check, check
rage is not the only ingredient for survival,
anger may soften the blow but will not harden the heart,
it will not erase your sin,
will not hand you a violin
to play your saddest tune in the ruin of her desire
to change you,
exchange you for the other one,
the one who will not measure the distance
between pleasure and pain,
who will not chain love to threat,
who will easily forget her corrosive words,
screamed into the dead of night,
relax, don't fight,
embrace your inner wings of wax,
        check
be like Icarus, sell your soul to the void
        check, check,
love, compassion, joy, equanimity
are reserved for those who know how to taper,
those who can crumple their heart like rice paper,
toss it in the garbage bin of passion,
separate the scream from the tone,
like Jesus' hands nailed to the cross,
the flesh from the metacarpal bone,

but what if the Buddha was wrong,
what if you are the noose tied to the tree
where she hangs from pain,
what if there is no gain in sitting in the burning coals,
what if by standing up and walking through,
you let her find someone who will love her better than you.

Burnt ink

What we don't know weaves a dark web
around our grey matter,
deflate our ego, a balloon let loose of air,
a leak in the plumbing,
secrets follow pipes, walls, beams, cracks,
find a way to the basement,
settle nicely on the decayed cement,
pool near the crazed furnace,
form a fastidious brown puddle
where thick mildew prospers,
       but we don't want to go there,
       we want to watch the next episode,
       not the rerun.

Why take the plunge
to the abyss of knowledge?
when you can stay in well aired
upper floors with reliable ceiling fans,
large windows looking onto
out of control peppermint bush.
A lingering incense of rare perfume on sheets
       worn out by lovers gone north,
       who left wet laundry in the machine
       and gaping holes in the heart.
Don't look into the well-known,
into what lights the big dipper,
what keeps the earth in orbit,
looking at the past
burns retinas with images of failure.

We will not ask
who did what to whom,
and who threw the first metaphoric punch,
a stone does not ask

the cold earth why it tilled over it,
a tree does not query the wind
why it tore its magnificent branches apart,
an oyster does not ask the sea
why it cracked open its cherished shell.

We destroy the evidence to keep afloat,
        burn it like the Mongols
        burnt the Alexandria library,
or was it Baghdad, the House of Wisdom,
where the Tigris like our thoughts,
is said to have turned black
from all the ink of charred books.
But where does all the burnt ink go?

Bernal Heights

From the top of winding hills,
the Bay city sleeps, in the distance
with its feet in the sea
a Red Hill above the tree line,
barren dirt
bare thoughts,
empty hands
open to the endless sky
to catch broken sunrays
fighting the morning fog
peace and war are worthy neighbors
white flags litter Hunters Point naval shipyards,
peace symbols on roofs of houses,
slanted to defy gravity.
When the flood comes to invent
and abolish the divine,
dogs bark and listen behind shut doors.

In the street window,
a woman appears to sleep
between semi-colons
and lethargic cats,
books covering her face,
stories of colonizers who spread disease,
and the ballet across the tribal land.
She says she can't sleep,
her fear wears her out,
the fear of not having fear.
She hugs the hazy early morning
as if it was her last,
flattens a pillow into her chest,
as if it was a loved one who died young.

Time folded around her
like a love letter with scuffed corners,
she waits naked by the window,
for a signal from the hill,
closes and opens her misty eyes,
as Bernal Heights awakens,

she says she found it,
then gives it all away,
this way it will never be lost.

NEAP TIDE

Witness I: Water Wings
For Aylan (Sept. 2, 2015)

Broken oars slam the
fickleness of the sea,

shredded life jackets, dreams
on the ocean floor,

a graveyard, the Mediterranean
where, as a child, I learned to swim,

flung in the sea to float aimlessly.
Buried with my ancestors in a

heartless orange brine.
Bite with sharp teeth the

goodbyes of a child
who never knew how

the liquid form turns
us into stones

with water wings.

Witness II: Still on

News crews gathering for that perfect shot
of the perfect baby lying on the beach,

in his perfect nappy quietude,
with perfect clothes still on,

still on,
still on,

the cameras are still on
insisting that he looks like he was sleeping.

We all know he is not sleeping,
we lie to stay afloat.

Cut to a rescuer's hands
out stretched in prayer,

on a forsaken beach,
a baby still in his red tee-shirt.

Why are we here?
What are we looking at?

his face in sand, turned to the dim Aegean,
the monster made from our watching,

swallowing his colorful dreams,
unaware of exit visas in Turkey,

entry visas to Canada.
He could not count to 4,

the distance between Bodrum and Kos,
where the tideline beat his small heart to silence,

without a visa.

Witness III: The Heart of Darkness

He's sleeping, not sleeping
unpredictable slumber engulfs a dejected coast,

oscillating waves, laps for naps,
a shoe made it to the other side,

the other shoe still on,
a tornado of grief turns our eyes into salt,

a volcano spitting the belly of
the earth into blinding lava.

This is how the world ends
with a click off,

to unsee, unwitness with eyelids closing
on a single surf lapping a small body,

slide the bayonets of our vision
back into their safe sheaths.

Forgive us little child,
– though we are not deserving of your forgiveness –

if one day we meet your beautiful eyes,
let it be a reminder of how

our conscience drowned,
with heavy limbs into a sea of apathy,

looking away sticks to our skin like wet sand.
While you are light, the twilight will

always break the heart of darkness.

All we Have

— "The present is all we have,"
you told me when we had nothing to lose,
and we wagered it all anyway,
on that fleeting moment by the sea,
staring at a still water surface,
wishing we had more than grains of sand
to grow our roots,
more than moving horizon lines,
to call home,
more than the tide
to sculpt our dreams,
but the present is never here
it is always a second too early
or a moment deferred
we spend our life in sullen regret or naïve hope
cursing walls for being too tall
airplanes for being too slow
mountain ranges for standing in the way
expecting tethered ropes to be strong and pull us close
and warm bed sheets to withstand the winter frost
lovers' time is a slivery violin
playing a grim gut wrenching tune
in the moment when no one is looking out for you
when you know your tribe lost its hunting ground
and you become a refugee
marching across a mountain of sorrow
looking for well-worn path to her body
drawing circles around an unmarked grave
where epic love stories go to die.

The Wind and the Wreckage

I am by the sea laying shattered on the Georgia Strait
  and I am a restful sun ray on glassy Spray lake in Canmore
    I am in the belly of the beast fighting with monsters
      and on the rooftop reading symbolist poetry
        I am the sleepless night standing sentry at the gates of desire
         and the door silently shutting on a silent gasp
          I am Icarus audaciously flying toward the sun
           and Orphic I am headed dreadfully to the Underworld
            to rescue a young boy's battered body

I'm the roadmap of truth with velvety blue edges
  and a vagrant blind oracle looking for answers in the trash pile of lies
    I am the intrepid lover who lights up her dusky sky
      and the torturer who whips frail skin to submission
        I am the final word that proves that I am
         and I, the silence of a lone cloud above a mountain of loss
          I am the waterway leading her through the reluctance of pleasure
        and the raised blade slicing the fallacy of oneness
         the contradiction and the end of contradiction
        I am the wind and the wreckage

Tuileries
For K

a kiss drips on your soft breast,
a night fog bruises,
shadows impersonate us on a warm bed
in the heat of Montmartre,

above streets with real people struggling real struggles
between African hairdressers and all night *boulanger*
frequented by nicely dressed taxi drivers.
In daytime, I showed you Paris above ground,
in all its splendor,
you found Paris underground with all its sleaze:
the boys cruising the lower hedges on the eastern edges
of *Jardin des Tuileries*,

tops and bottoms closing the gap between
a geo-locator and the bulging lust,
casually dropping their pants at forbidden green gates,
distance in the bush is temporary – your intrepid body says
between fingers and
the expiration of breath,
a scandal awaits –
scandal from *Skandalon,* a "snare"
trapped under your sheer shawl,
my body counting strokes,

and people, looking, sitting, standing,
panting, gasping,
waves ruffle the wind under an anonymous tree,
groove me at liquescent angles
under the watchful eyes of young hustlers,
and sluggish park cleaners.
Lust turns us into amphibians

diving to find the indulgence of rare gems in the body,
between frozen bronze statues with faded names,
engraved in haste,
the taste of pleasure *en plein air*, the apogee
of luscious infamy, delicious ignominy.
Your triumphant smile at the end,

the dead giveaway,

your terra nostra,
is a sea you invented for me,
what separates pleasure from shame,
a vessel I did not know I can sail,
à l'estime d'une passion that
so wants us to name it,
claim it, untame it.
Your Twillery.

Break Fall

we practiced break
falling
        break downs,

        free falls,
I coasted the fall of
broken promises.
After all hell broke loose

broke stride
broke the mold
broke habits

        breaking new grounds
break out in a rash of memory

        breaking the silence
breaking the code of your armor
breaking
        spells
making a break for it from
the prison house of
        indifference
the straw and
        camel's back too

Sticks and stones may break my...
        but no words.

Streets empty of disturbances,
my mourning started
        before you woke up
before geography

        became fiction,
before I put my hand on your heart
to feel the shape of a beat
before I told you:
you are

the Damascus of my sorrow
the Baghdad of my grief,
the Beirut of my lament.

When love begins, no one counts
        the blows,
the breaks, the takes,
the strokes,
        the bruises confused
with normal skin hues,
the ruses that turn
        abuses
into a holy book

        of affection.

How long it took to read it,
        to find you in it,
to dog ear your pages inside

        its pallid papers?
And how fast it took to burn it,
tear the pages
        where your name appeared
and disappeared in pale

        charred ink?

How does winning an argument become
more important than winning a heart?

The Naked Arbutus
For Carol

"F hearts L," carved
in this midget red arbutus,

bewailing its fallen bark.
A Salty Island lies beneath, chatting with the sea.

Animated characters tapping on silky tree trunk
the rhythm of our disappearance.

Living woods hold the beat in their mossy branches,
phantoms only visible to some,

they take on different shapes
as they are gazed upon,

sculpt our vision, mold our inner seas.
We do not have a heart in this story,

we are neither L nor F,
our names are carved on brittle shores,

our past, captured in upward tree roots
too short to reach the heavens.

What did the naked arbutus
whisper to the bald eagle,

beelining to Mount Maxwell from
the top of Reginald Hill?

"Not all those who are lost
are looking to be found."

Scraps

I have scribbled so many verses
        on so many scraps of paper,
        post-it notes,
        grocery lists,
        pizza flyers,
        the back of student essays,
        on old agendas,
        on Bible pages ripped from seedy hotels,
fragment of a *poeisis* no one will read,
a life in tattered words,
legends of undeserving anti-heroes,
leafy echoes of insignificance,
hope posing as the grim reaper,
logs of lovers gone on faded yellow paper,
wilted petals, broken stems,
canvas of onion peels,
napkins stained with coffee, refilled by grumpy waitresses,
dead wood, petrified branches,
sand bars where time stood still,
then lied down to rest,
lapsed in three continents
where love never stays long enough to become a home.

Spiders climbing the walls of our brick heart,
chronically – a Sisyphus patiently restarting the climb until
we forget how far the top is from the ground,
a wager between equally problematic bets
– to be alone and to be a loan to someone else,
who wants you for your skillfully folded laundry,
        for your way with words,
        for your upper body strength,
        for your accent,
        for your indecent disposition,
        for how you speak to the construction workers,
        for being the only mirror that reflects a fractured reality.

It begins with thousands scrap papers,
notes for a thousand tomorrows,

and it ends with a singular torn yesterday,
where you shut the door and went to sleep,
bequest me your dream, wrapped
in an old newspaper,
where fragments of my next poem will begin.

"Tilted Ladders"

> "*The siege is a waiting period*
> *Waiting on the tilted ladder in the middle of the storm*"
> -Mahmoud Darwish

Hanging suspended on bridges to nowhere,
below, a fast-moving river that may or

may not dump in the Atlantic, how should I know?
geography retires when you're transient.

Leonard Cohen wailing from the one
working speaker... it must be illegal to feel this way,

between two lands, two homes, two guarded duty frees,
where you can buy cigarettes and rum, but no smile.

I am in a state of siege between two borders,
following orders to move or stay, go or wait,

advance, retreat,
by a dog and his human in riot gear.

A 49th parallel paralleling patrols of petrified purity,
his jaw is our fate,

he wanted to know how we relate,
"How are you associated? MAA'M?

'Partners,' I said to sooth his homophobic discontent,
"Like, business PARTNERS?" he asks,

'No, like bed partners,' I replied,
he feels more justified than ever to dislike

this unruly dyke who is about to be arrested
for thinking of your breasts on the Rainbow Bridge.

They are exceptionally perky perched

83

persnickety in my punctilious right palm,

a controlled substance, a forbidden delight, a slight
of hand for the grand chief of this land.

You and I are big sista's, terroristas, laying in wait
in the eye of two storms, fueling the twista',

drafty dodgers, conscious resisters,
the salt in the cake,

the bleeding raw steak, the reason the law
gets out of bed in the morning.

You, at least were born in New Scotland,
on a beach engraved on red fifty-dollar bills,

me, I am naturalized Canadian,
unnatural, denatural, endentured to a document

24 pages long, with the head of the Queen,
and her heirs, I must swear to,

staring at my sacrilegious dare.
I was flung into this world in the seventh city

of jasmine and incense, on a rocky shore,
the pearl of the orient

disoriented, rented, indented, ointed,
with cedar bark from a holy valley

of saints dancing among demons.
And I am *bented*, accented, can't repent it

from what torments them about difference.
They hide their non-sense behind loaded guns.

In a world governed by terror,
queer love becomes a form of resistance,

trapped between two stances,
two flags, two banks, two waterfalls, two watch towers,

two chances to fall into a raging river of hate,
jaw spurned, upturned, interned, churned

by the pure-bred German shepherd
with a charming white canine smile.

Left to Write

And now there is nothing left to write,
everything is encrypted in an image of
an image, inside a kaleidoscope
where the original is lost, said Baudrillard,
or was it Abu Tammam?
Peddling meaning to those who can afford it,
divorced from those who can understand,
hording parables like precious paper after the last tree is cut,
rationed water after the drought.
When did we become a wheel barrow
for the rich in cash but poor in imagination?
selling words as passports with prized visas
to transport their bankrupt souls
between two beacons of cynicism?
The old president is painting pictures,
worn out by the darkness of dropping bombs,
he went seeking light at the tip of a brush,
for a chiaroscuro of self-forgiveness.

The poet is weary of being broke,
he took a job tending to their gardens,
where he buried his unfinished manuscript
under the leafy autumn, by the shiny white fence,
where only the overfed dog is allowed to void.
The Boss said: "you're overqualified for trimming trees,"
and gave him a job in the kitchen
stuffing mushrooms with the precision of a bomb maker,
ensuring the shine on the fungus is preserved,
with slippery roundness streaming
across their gold-plated tables.
The ladies of the mansion shrug their
narrow shoulders, draped with cashmere,
– "Tibetan Shahtoosh," to be precise,
around their neck, the screams of ibex can still be heard.
Is that all poetry has to say about the triumph of capital?

Icarus

"Icarus was not burnt. He has not yet returned"
                                    - Adonis (Ali Ahmad Said)

falling taught me the meaning of flight
a precipice taught me the meaning of balance
a desert taught me the meaning of plenty
a wave taught me the meaning of grief
a rope taught me the meaning of breathing
an ice storm taught me the meaning of fire
a leaf taught me the meaning of dying
a seashell taught me the meaning of listening
a shot glass taught me the meaning of deception
a sunray taught me the meaning of blindness
a mirror taught me the meaning of lying
a landmine taught me the meaning of compassion
ashes taught me the meaning of victory
a shipwreck taught me the meaning of survival
a scar taught me the meaning of forgiving
a pomegranate taught me the meaning of seduction
a bullet taught me the meaning of trust
leaving taught me the meaning of home

ACKNOWLEDGEMENTS

Some of the poems in this collection have previously appeared in the following: *Bookend Review,* "Water Skipper's Stone"; *Lavender Review*, "Tilted Ladder"; *Linden Avenue,* "Witness II"; *Gravel Literary Magazine*, "Auguste"; *40 Below Anthology*, "Narcissus"; *Skin2Skin Journal*, "Bernal Heights"; *Gutter Eloquence*, "Icarus"; *Poetry Quarterly*, "All We Have"; *Yes, Poetry,* "Plimsoll Lines I"; *The Toronto Quarterly*, "Liquid Caresses."

ABOUT THE AUTHOR

Donia Mounsef was born and lived in Beirut, Lebanon until the age of 19. She is a Canadian-Lebanese poet, playwright and dramaturge. She splits her time between Toronto and Edmonton where she teaches theatre and poetry at the University of Alberta. She is the author of a poetry chapbook, Slant of Arils (Damaged Goods Press, 2015). Her writing has been published and anthologized in print and online in The Toronto Quarterly, Bluestem, Yes Poetry, Gutter Eloquence, Poetry Quarterly, Skin 2 Skin, Iris Brown, Lavender Review, Linden Avenue, Gravel, 40 Below Anthology, among others. Her performance poetry and plays have been performed on stages in

Toronto, Montréal, Vancouver, Edmonton, and New Haven.

CPSIA information can be obtained
at www.ICGtesting.com
Printed in the USA
LVHW04s1757120818
586745LV00005B/718/P